W9-AUA-956

Planning and Directing a Wedding:
Guidelines for a Bride, Mother, and Director

By Dorothy Burdashaw Parrish

Fourth Printing, January 2002

Library of Congress Cataloging - in - Publication Data

ISBN 0-9656331-0-1

printed by

Miller Printing Co., Inc.

Augusta, Georgia

This book is dedicated to the Glory of God and in honor of Dr. Robert Parrish, my husband of forty-two years.

This book was inspired by the Trinity-on-the-Hill United Methodist Church of Augusta, Georgia wedding committee, where I developed my first love of directing weddings. Also, to my two wonderful daughters, Joy Simmons and Cindy Center, both of whom instilled in me the wonderful bond developed between a daughter and mother during the planning of their weddings.

The author gratefully acknowledges the assistance of Jennie Elliott in the production of this book.

Author's Notes

Eighteen years ago, my first daughter became engaged. When the excitement of the engagement was over, it suddenly dawned on me that we needed to start planning her wedding. How do we start? What comes first? Believe me, I had some very anxious moments. I started reading books to help us, but the more I read, the more confused I became. I was looking for two things: a simple plan to follow, and someone to direct the wedding.

A friend of mine was on the wedding committee at my church. She was my life saver. From the very beginning, she explained that this day should be the happiest day of a bride's life, as well as her mother's. Without planning, I knew it could fall short of the perfect wedding my daughter had always dreamed of having. So, for the next six months I worked out my plans, and my friend directed the wedding.

The big day came, and the whole family enjoyed every minute of it...even me. For the next five years, I was a member of the wedding committee in my church. I gave workshops in several churches in the Augusta, Georgia area enabling them to start their wedding committees. My enthusiasm was contagious. News began to spread about the weddings I had directed. My friends began to ask me to help with their daughters' weddings. So, I started going to other churches to help. I found that most churches have wedding committees to help the mother and bride with the rehearsal and wedding, but they do not direct the wedding. This bothered me. So, I have used my eighteen years of experience in planning and directing weddings to write up these guidelines. Hopefully the purpose of this book will be to help the mother and bride plan the wedding and give a wedding committee member or any interested person a method on how to direct.

Planning and Directing a Wedding

Planning Outline: First Session

Two Weeks to complete arrangements

Minister
Church
Florist
Reception
Caterer
Cake
Photographer
Video Tape
Music

Session One

To be successful in conducting a wedding, the director must be involved in all aspects of the wedding. Not only is it important for the director to give advice, but also to bond with the bride and mother. They will find the director is their security and sounding board to talk over all their arrangements and problems as the months go by. It would be nice to have a year before the wedding, which makes it easier to schedule the wedding date the bride and groom would like to have. June is still the most popular month for brides. Church calendars fill up very quickly for June and December. If a year is impossible, six months is desirable. Six months is not too soon to reserve the church, select the location for the reception and engage the services you need.

I like to have three sessions with the bride and mother to complete the planning of the wedding. In the first session, we will go over plans for the minister, church, florist, reception, caterer, cake, photographer, the video tape, and music.

● *Setting the Date*

The bride and groom must set up a wedding date and time with the cooperation of the minister. This time and date must be agreeable with the groom's family. At this time, the couple should set up a counseling session with the minister of the church. Guest ministers must be approved by the minister of the church where the wedding will be performed. Honorarium is paid directly to the minister and is given to him by the best man either prior to or immediately following the ceremony.

When the date is established, the minister will check the church calendar. At this time, the reservations may be made with the church. Most all churches have guides and policies for weddings performed in the church. A list of these policies should be picked up by the bride along with the wedding contracts for the florist, photographer, and caterer (if the reception is held at the church). If the wedding is somewhere other than a church, reservations must be made at this time.

● *Fabulous Flowers*

As for the florist, two or three should be contacted, unless the mother would like to use her regular florist. If this is not the case, the director can usually give some helpful advice from working with many florists. Here are some helpful tips: 1) Have the florists express their creative ideas. 2) Ask about the flowers that are available during the month of your wedding. 3) Ask for pictures of the weddings they have done. 4) Ask for an up-coming wedding date so you can go by the church and see their work. 5) By all means, get prices on what you want from them. I find that the prices sometimes differ a great deal from one florist to the next, but remember the cheapest is *not* always the best. You decide on the one who is best for you. Keep decorations simple; some of the most beautiful and elegant weddings I have directed had the most simple arrangements of flowers and decorations. A well organized florist will make a diagram showing you where all the decorations will be placed at the church and reception.

The florist should be available before the wedding to light candles (unless ushers are used), pin on boutonnieres and corsages, and to direct the bride and attendants on how to hold their bouquets. After the wedding, the florist should help in any way with the flowers for pictures. They might not be needed, but it is nice to offer. This is a convenient service, for they are already there to remove the decorations from the church. Do not ask a florist to take an arrangement from the church to the reception; decorations for each of these should be handled separately. Finally, the florist will give a list of flower responsibilities to the bride and groom so that each family member understands what is expected of them. Remember, florist, a satisfied customer is the best advertisement you could have for the future.

- *Reception Options*

If the reception is not at the church, the bride and mother should look at several places to hold the reception. They should decide together on the place that is best for them. The location and rental price should certainly be considered.

- *Creative and Cost-effective Catering*

The next step is very important: finding a good caterer. If you already have one in mind, talk with the caterer and ask for prices. I think it is necessary to check with two or more caterers to compare prices. Remember, the food is the most expensive part of a wedding. Shop carefully; be satisfied, and talk it over with your director. If you decide on a country club for the reception, you will be using the food prepared by the club. There are still prices to consider according to the food you select. Like a florist, a well organized caterer will make a diagram of the room placing each table used on the diagram. If the arrangement is not satisfactory, the diagram can be changed immediately until you are well pleased. Again, remember to shop wisely.

Another very important part of the reception is the wedding cake. The cake is a work of art! Many bakeries can help you. Sometimes you can find people who do nothing but make wedding cakes; I have found many are excellent. They take great pride in their work. Many times the director knows of such a person. Cakes are usually not too expensive. Fresh flowers on a cake are very beautiful and elegant. But remember, the cake must not only be beautiful, but appealing to the taste buds. You want a wedding cake that your guests will enjoy and remember. The bride's cake can be any shape, but usually round and white, whereas the groom's is square or long and chocolate. The top of the bride's cake can be lifted off, saved, frozen, and enjoyed on the couple's first anniversary.

- *Perfect Pictures*

The next subject to discuss is the photographer. Pictures are very important, for when the wedding is over the only things left are pictures, and of course, beautiful memories. Take time selecting a photographer. Again, talk with several of them. Be satisfied that you understand what they have to offer you. Communication is very important here. I have found several brides that were disappointed in the selection of their photographer because of a lack of communication in the beginning. Look at the photographers' work and compare prices. Your wedding director has experience with photographers; ask for some advice. One helpful tip: stress to the photographer to take as many photos as possible before the ceremony. The pictures involving the bride and groom are taken after the ceremony. Sometimes picture taking can delay the bride and groom from getting to the reception at a reasonable time.

Most people want to video tape their wedding. Most churches can give you a list of people who video weddings. Talk with several people, and be sure they understand exactly what you are expecting. Again, communication is very important. Video taping is best accomplished from the balcony. Shop wisely for this service.

- *Memorable Music*

As for music, the church's organist is the best person to play for your wedding. If this is not possible, the organist will have a list of other qualified organists. Also, if you do not have a vocalist, the organist can suggest several for you to choose and hire. Meet with the organist and vocalist several weeks before the wedding to select the music. If the wedding and/or reception is in a church, all music must be approved by the Minister of Music before the rehearsal. Fees for the organist and vocalist are paid directly to the individual.

When we have thoroughly discussed each topic, as a director, I like to give the bride and mother two weeks to make all contacts. After the time and the date of the wedding is decided, you need to establish who will be fulfilling each service. Do not hesitate to call a service to ask any questions before you make deposits to hold a date. After you have made the deposits, the bride and mother will check over final arrangements several months before the wedding.

Planning Outline: Second Session

Next two weeks to complete arrangements

Bridesmaids
Junior bridesmaids
Ring bearer
Flower girl
Groomsmen
Engagement announcement
Wedding announcement
Invitations
Shower and wedding gifts
Selecting china, crystal, silver

Session Two

The bride and mother may want to talk with the director about a problem during the two weeks. At the end of the two weeks, getting together for a second session is important. At this time, all of the first session planning must be completed. Again, be sure you are completely satisfied with each service you need for the wedding. After this, let the professionals you have hired take over their jobs. Unless a question comes up, you do not need to contact them until you confirm the final arrangements.

The topics for the second session are as follows: bridesmaids, junior bridesmaids, ring bearer, flower girl, grooms-men, engagement announcement, invitations, shower and wedding gifts, and selection of china, crystal, and silver. Sometimes the wedding party has already been asked, but it is still important to discuss it.

● *Selecting the Wedding Party*

First of all, do not ask everyone you know to be a bridesmaid. All attendants should be chosen because of their closeness to the bride and/or groom. You may choose sisters, cousins, or very close friends to be in your wedding. If you have both a maid of honor (unmarried) and a matron of honor (married), either one may attend you; they share equal honors. Usually, the maid of honor stands closest to the bride. Her duties are to take the bride's flowers, hand her the ring, fix her veil and train, and to assist her in any way. The girls must be willing to buy the dress that the bride has selected. When selecting a dress, choose one that your friends can wear later. They do not enjoy buying a dress that they will *never* wear again. Try to consider them.

Young friends, sisters, or other young relatives can be junior bridesmaids. They should wear the same style dress as the bridesmaids; however, if they are between eight and ten, you may consider dressing them in white.

If you choose to have a ring bearer, his suit may be made or found at a formal wear rental store. He will carry a little white pillow with two wedding rings tied on top. Do not use the real rings on the pillow; they should be with the best man and the bride's honored attendant. I would suggest that you do not have a ring bearer below the age of five, as younger children are sometimes reluctant to go down the aisle. If you are not careful, they can take away from the wedding instead of adding to it.

The flower girl can wear an exact miniature of the bridesmaid's dress or not. I like to see the flower girl dressed entirely different from the bridesmaids. A beautiful french lace dress with a lot of smocking and embroidered roses on it is so beautiful on a little girl. She should carry a white basket with dried rose petals in it to drop along the aisle. Dried or silk rose petals have become very popular to use, for fresh petals can stain the carpet. Here again, the flower girl should be at least five years old.

The groom needs a best man and groomsmen that equal the same number of bridesmaids and honored attendants. If the wedding guest list is very large, two or more ushers may be asked. It is necessary to have a groomsman for every fifty guests. In some cases, the best man can help usher for about twenty minutes, but I do not encourage this. The groom and bride should decide on where the groomsmen get their tuxedos. They should go to a reliable formal wear rental place and make their selections based on the many available models in the store. Go to several stores and decide together on which you believe will give you the best service. Your wedding director has certainly had a lot of experience with this service. I think the traditional black is elegant and in good taste.

● *Engagement Announcement*

The engagement announcement is usually put in the newspaper three months before the wedding. The bride can pick up the engagement and wedding forms for the newspaper at any time. I would suggest you get them soon, fill them out so they will be ready to be given to the newspaper at the appropriate time.

● *Invitations*

When selecting invitations for your wedding, choose one that is traditional. Pictures are not usually used; sometimes they can take away from the invitation. Engraved invitations are beautiful, but expensive. Printed invitations are so similar to engraving that most people cannot tell the difference, and you can save a lot of money. The printer will give you the date on which you must place your order so you will have the proper time to complete addressing your invitations. At this time, you will need to order your napkins, stationary, cards, informals, etc. When you receive your invitations from the printer, you will find a brochure giving you instructions on how to properly address and mail envelopes. There are two important tips to remember: use *black ink* and write the *full name* of a guest when you are addressing envelopes. I received a beautiful invitation written in calligraphy with "Dr. and Mrs. Robert A. Parrish" written on the envelope. I know the mother spent a lot of money to have these invitations written, but all I saw was the initial jumping at me off the envelope. If you do not know the middle name, just omit it. When invitations have not been sent, announcements may be sent after the wedding.

Now is the time to begin the invitation list. This is a very hard job. You should not invite everyone you know, but you do not want to leave out someone you have been associated with through school, work, etc. Work on this list every day. When you think of a person during the day, stop and write down the name. Sometimes, the mother of the bride will limit the groom's parents to a certain number of guests. They will probably not be inviting as many as the bride, but they should be allowed to have as many guests as they would like if at all possible.

I would suggest you buy two file boxes and three-by-five index cards to be alphabetized in these boxes. One will be for the bride's mother, and one for the groom's mother. Compile your guest list as soon as possible, and encourage the groom's mother to do the same. An example of a card appears on the next page:

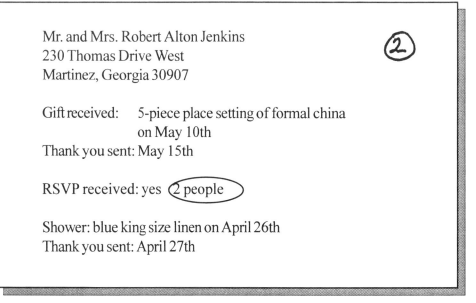

Figure 1: Sample File Card

You will notice that I have circled the number of people who will be coming to the wedding and placed the number circled in the right hand corner of the index card. This is the number to count when you give a final estimate to the caterer two weeks before the wedding. Your caterer will charge you for the total number you give them, so try to have the correct estimate of guests.

The groom's mother should complete her file and return it to the bride at least six weeks before the wedding. Two weeks should be allowed for addressing invitations. The invitations need to be in the mail four weeks before the wedding. Stamped RSVP notes are very nice to inclose in your invitations. Most people are every good about returning these notes. When you receive the returned RSVP note, record this information in your alphabetized card box. It is very important to keep two files, because the groom's mother can help answer questions that might come up about her list. Also, she will be very helpful when you are arriving at the final count for the caterer.

Before leaving the subject of invitations, I would like to address the subject of shower and wedding gifts. Gifts are given to the bride and groom, but the bride usually writes all of the thank you notes. As soon as a gift is given, the bride should acknowledge immediately with a very sincere hand-written thank you note. It is very disappointing to receive a thank you note when the couple has been married so long that the guests cannot remember the gift they sent. Sometimes, the thank you note is the only means by which one knows the couple have received a gift. So, write your notes early to show appreciation for the beautiful gifts you have received.

• *Selecting China, Crystal, and Silver*

Before the invitations are sent, the bride and groom should select china, crystal, silver, linens, and other gifts from stores. You should register at all department and jewelry stores and stores that have a bridal service in your community. In this way, you have given your guests many places to shop, as some people like to shop at a particular place.

Planning Outline: Third Session

Mothers' dresses
Rehearsal dinner
Book of important numbers
Gifts for attendants
Out of town guests
Wedding dress

Session Three

In the third session, we need to talk about mothers' dresses, the rehearsal dinner, the book of numbers, gifts for attendants, out of town guests, the bride's dress, and any problems that need to be addressed. After this session, we will have completed the planning.

• *Mothers' Dresses*

The mother of the bride should select her dress first. She should choose a dress in a style and color that complements the bride's gown and the bridesmaids' attire. As soon as possible, advise the groom's mother of your choice so that she may select a similar look. The mothers should wear the same length gowns. Nothing should be worn to detract from the bride.

• *Rehearsal Dinner*

The rehearsal dinner is the responsibility of the groom's family, but anyone can host the meal as long as the groom's parents are agreeable. The mother of the bride can help with the arrangements if the groom's parents are out of town. The dinner is usually held after the rehearsal. The groom's parents should invite all members of the wedding party and their escorts, parents and immediate family of the bridal couple, the minister and his wife, the wedding director and escort and any other special friends. Out of town guests are usually included in the guest list. Any seating arrangement is suitable, but the bride, groom, and bride's parents should all eat together at the head table. Do not use place cards; let your guests sit together as they choose. You want them to enjoy a relaxing evening. Try to keep the rehearsal party limited to three hours. The dinner is usually the night before the wedding, and everyone needs to get a good night's rest before the big event. Through the years, I have seen several groomsmen who were a little tired the day of the wedding. Too much partying, don't you think? The groom can usually control his groomsmen in this matter.

- ***The Book of Numbers***

The mother of the bride needs to make a book of important numbers and information to help keep the next few months running smoothly. I would suggest using a file box, notebook, or a small photo book with index cards inserted in the frames instead of pictures. The photo book is the one I enjoy. Here is an example of how to keep your book:

Open Photo Book

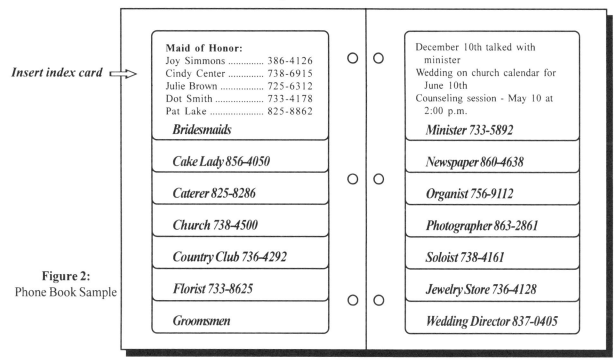

Insert index card ⇒

Maid of Honor:
Joy Simmons 386-4126
Cindy Center 738-6915
Julie Brown 725-6312
Dot Smith 733-4178
Pat Lake 825-8862

Bridesmaids

Cake Lady 856-4050

Caterer 825-8286

Church 738-4500

Country Club 736-4292

Florist 733-8625

Groomsmen

December 10th talked with
   minister
Wedding on church calendar for
   June 10th
Counseling session - May 10 at
   2:00 p.m.

Minister 733-5892

Newspaper 860-4638

Organist 756-9112

Photographer 863-2861

Soloist 738-4161

Jewelry Store 736-4128

Wedding Director 837-0405

Figure 2:
Phone Book Sample

You can find this kind of photo book at any camera store. I like it because it is small and you can add as many pages as you need. Each card flips up so you can insert the next card. Here is an example of one card:

1. Made deposit to hold date – $100.00 on January 22nd

2. Talk about arrangements and decorations April 15th

3. Final plans and talk June 2nd – paid $500.00 on bill

4. Touch base one week before wedding June 15th

5. Paid final bill on June 17th

Florist   *733-8625*

Figure 3: Sample Photo Book Card

Again, if you like, you can keep your cards in a file box. You cannot imagine how much you will use this book. Not only are the numbers before you, but the amount and date of your deposits, date to confirm all plans, and any other information you might need. The last week before the wedding, you can flip through the cards and touch base with each service. You will probably have other numbers, but these numbers should definitely be in your book: minister, church office or wherever the ceremony will be held, place of reception, florist, caterer, cake maker or bakery, photographer, organist, vocalist, video tape director, bridesmaids, groomsmen, newspaper, all the stores that have the gift selections, store with bridesmaids' dresses, mothers' dresses and formal wear rental store for groomsmen. This book will help immensely in keeping everything running smoothly in the last few months before the wedding. I would suggest alphabetizing this book for easy reference.

Before finishing the third session, three subjects should be addressed: gifts for attendants, out of town guests, and the bride's dress.

● *Gifts for Attendants*

The bride should give her attendants either something she would like them to wear in the wedding such as earrings, a necklace, or a little personal gift they can enjoy and would be a lasting memory of this special bride. The bride may want to give gifts to such people as the organist, soloist, and others who will be in the wedding, provided these are not paid participants. Personalized gifts such as cuff links, pen sets, key chains, mugs, or even a small brass bedside clock make wonderful groomsmen gifts. The bride and groom should shop together and put a lot of thought into their gifts. In April and May, I have noticed some stores have beautiful displays of appropriate gifts for bridesmaids and groomsmen. This is very helpful when selecting gifts. Choose something that you would like to receive if you were in that person's wedding. The gifts to the bridesmaids should be given at the bridesmaids' luncheon. This luncheon is given by one of the bride's honored attendants, a relative, or a close friend. All the bridesmaids and mothers are invited, and it is usually the day before the wedding. The gifts to the groomsmen should be given at the bachelor party or rehearsal dinner.

- ### *Out of town Guests*

Out of town guest are very special. If possible, it is nice to have some of the guests stay in private homes. Some of your close friends may offer a room in their home. However, many guests would like hotel recommendations. Some hotels will quote a special rate. Check with several hotels for information, and take into consideration the price and location. When you have made a choice, reserve a block of rooms to be held for your guests. This will be a help to the hotel and your guests when they call to make reservations. The day before the out of town guests arrive, leave a little basket at the registration desk for each guest with a note from you, maps of the city, cookies, candy or anything you think would be appropriate. If you are creative, make something. Remember, they came for your special day; let them know you care.

- ### *Selecting a Wedding Dress*

Selecting a wedding dress is a special time between mother and daughter. The mother is there for emotional support, and encouragement. The relationship grows stronger as they plan for the wedding day together. I remember so well when our first daughter, Joy, got married. It was ten days after Bob and I had our twenty-fifth wedding anniversary. She chose to wear my wedding gown. What a thrill it was to see our first little girl dressed in my wedding gown coming down the aisle with her father. Think seriously about the possibility of wearing your mother's wedding gown. It is an honor for both mother and daughter.

The day Cindy, our second daughter, and I went looking for a gown was a day we will never forget. Our goal was to find the perfect dress. I think all little girls want to feel like Cinderella on their wedding day. Encouragement and support between the mother and bride is very important. Make this time of buying the wedding gown a very special time.

The first two sessions should be finished in about a month. The things we talked about in the third session will take longer. Try to finish up as many as you can in the second month. If you do, hooray for you! This will give you more time to have fun and enjoy your wedding.

All of the planning is now complete. If there are any problems, talk them over with the wedding director. You should not have to talk with any of your services until the date when you confirm your plans, unless a question comes up before then.

• *Confirming your Plans*

Two weeks before the wedding, the caterer will want a final estimate of the number of guests expected at the reception. The week of the wedding, you should contact your florist, caterer, organist, soloist, and photographer just to touch base with them. Be sure they understand not only the date, but the time they need to be working. It is always best to make a final check.

It is nice to have a director to go through the wedding, but with the information I have given you, you could take care of all the planning. The secret of planning a wedding is to be completely satisfied with the people you have hired to take care of the services you need. Let them take over and release you from the pressure of details and decisions. The professionals will work with the bride and mother enabling everything to run smoothly. With this burden over, you will find yourself having a wonderful time and looking forward to the big day.

● *Suggestions for the Mother and the Bride*

I would like to suggest a few things to the mother and bride. To the mother, remember to always respect the wishes of your daughter and her fiancé. It is their wedding, not yours. The couple is looking to you for guidance, and they get upset with so many decisions that have to be made. Be patient with them. To the bride, your mother has not only a lot of preparations to make, but she is also realizing she is going to have to share you with a new family of relatives. Work together with a lot of love and understanding. Finally to the mother and bride, as you both work through your planning, try to keep the groom's family informed. Sometimes they can feel like outsiders. The groom's mother will certainly feel left out if she is not included in the planning. Through the years, I have seen families divided and hardly speaking before the wedding. Communication is extremely important between the families. Starting off with misunderstandings sometimes causes wounds that never heal. Do not let this happen to your families. They probably will never be close, but you want them to get along. There will be other occasions through life that they will come together, perhaps the best being the wonderful grandchildren that can come into your life and steal your hearts. Make a good beginning for everyone.

Before we continue into directing a wedding, let's be sure these items have been checked off our list:

____ 1. Minister
____ 2. Church
____ 3. Reception
____ 4. Florist
____ 5. Caterer
____ 6. Cake

___ 7. Photographer
___ 8. Music
___ 9. Video tape
___ 10. Wedding dress purchased
___ 11. Mothers' dresses purchased
___ 12. Bridesmaids' dresses purchased
___ 13. Ring bearer - flower girl attire selected
___ 14. Groomsmen tuxedos rented
___ 15. Book of numbers made
___ 16. Invitations ordered
___ 17. Selection of china, crystal, and silver
___ 18. Rehearsal and dinner arrangements made
___ 19. Gifts for attendants bought
___ 20. Accommodations for out of town guests
___ 21. Engagement announcement already in paper
___ 22. Wedding announcement written and ready for paper
___ 23. Thank you notes mailed for all wedding and shower gifts so far

Remember: do not use stationary with your new initials until after you marry. Some brides have their notes ready for their mother to mail the day after the wedding. You do not need to write notes the week before the wedding, unless you find some extra time. Many brides have told me that they enjoy writing notes the last week to keep their minds occupied. That is a good method to keep from getting nervous. If this will help you, do it. Remember, after you get married it will be harder to get your notes written.

___ 24. Arrangements made for all transportation for guests (if necessary) and a car or limousine for bride and groom

Contracts for florist, photographer, and caterer (if at the church) should be signed and returned to the church office. All church requirements and outside fees need to be fulfilled. Now is the time to spend with the wedding director and committee. These are the people that are going to make all of the planning and preparation so far come together for a beautiful wedding ceremony.

Directing Outline: Fourth Session

Fill out form
Ask questions
Make diagram
Processional
Recessional
Escorts
Wedding Sample
Reception

Session Four

The church's wedding committee members are very dedicated and will assist in any way. For instance, they can call members involved in the wedding. All churches should have this service. I started my love of directing weddings as a committee member. Many times directors are missing from wedding committees. So my goal in the next pages of this book is to teach how to become a wedding director. I have used this method for eighteen years and found it to be successful.

About two weeks before the wedding, the bride, mother, and director should meet at the church. The director will have given a form to be filled out before the meeting. The bride, mother and groom's mother need to discuss this information and complete the form together. On this form, I only use the first name of the people unless two people have the same name, and then I write the first letter of their last name. Here is an example of a form. I have added names to let you see how it works.

BRIDE
Cindy

MAID OF HONOR
Mary Kay

MATRON OF HONOR
Joy

BRIDESMAIDS
Betty C.
Jo Ann
Beth
May
Betty K.

FLOWER GIRL
Bailie

BRIDE'S PARENTS
Dot and Bob

TO ESCORT GRANDMOTHERS
Gene and Blake C.

TO ESCORT BRIDE'S MOTHER
Blake C.

GROOM
Eric

BEST MAN
Kevin

GROOMSMEN
Gene
Blake C.
Kelly
Henry
Blake T.
Joe
Extra ushers*

RING BEARER
Barrett

GROOM'S PARENTS
Jo and Jack

TO ESCORT GRANDMOTHERS
Kelly and Henry

TO ESCORT GROOM'S MOTHER
Henry

*Extra ushers are needed if the guest list is very large. An usher is needed for every fifty guests attending.

Read over the completed form with the bride and mother. With this information, ask the following questions:

1. Do you want the minister, groom, and best man to come down the aisle or enter from the side of the altar?
2. Do you want groomsmen on the right and bridesmaids on the left, or interspersed on both sides?
3. Are there certain bridesmaids and groomsmen you would like coupled together?
4. Tell me approximately the tallest to the shortest groomsmen, so you can have the tallest on the end unless he is the best man. Use the same idea for the bridesmaids.
5. Tell me which bridesmaids look best with which groomsmen.
6. Do you want the extra ushers (if there are any) in the wedding party or to remain in the back to see that late-comers are directed to sit in the back, unescorted?
7. Do you want the ring bearer and flower girl to come down the aisle together or separately?
8. Do you want the groomsmen to process in pairs or single file?
9. Do you want the bridesmaids to process in pairs or in single file?
10. Would you like the attendants to process in couples? This way is pretty for a very large wedding.
11. Is there a very special friend or relative that you would like escorted just before the grandmothers are escorted into the church?
12. Are there any solos before the mothers are escorted into the church?
13. Are there any solos after the mothers are seated before the wedding party enters?
14. Would you like your father to escort your mother into the church?
15. Would you like to give your mother a rose before you and your father process to the altar?
16. Would you like to give the groom's mother a rose as you and your new husband recess from the church?
17. Will you be lighting a unity candle?
18. Do you want your mother and the groom's mother to light a candle before being escorted to their pews?
19. Do you (the bride's mother) want to stand as the bride and her father process down the aisle? The bride's

mother is the cue for the guests to stand, but most of the time, they stand anyway. If you do not want to stand, the minister can inform the congregation before the bridal party starts.

20. Will there be a single or a double ring ceremony?

21. Do you want the groom's parents to follow your parents coming out of the church? If the groom's father is the best man, then he will go back for the groom's mother.

23. Do you want the grandmothers to be escorted out or remain in their pews?

After these questions are asked and you have written notes with the help of the bride, make a diagram. The time you spend here with the bride is very important. The bride knows how she would like to see the wedding party at the altar. You are learning from her help. Making this diagram is the most important part of directing.

In the following pages, I will give you two diagrams to look at using the names from the first form. Look back at that form so you can see how I worked with the names. Remember, use the information the bride gives you to come up with these diagrams. After I have given you the diagram, I have listed the line-up coming in at the back of the church and the line-up going out of the church at the altar.

First, let's look at a simple diagram. Suppose the bride wants all of her bridesmaids on the bride's side, and all the groomsmen on the groom's side. Your diagram and line-ups would look like these:

ALTAR – Bridesmaids on one side

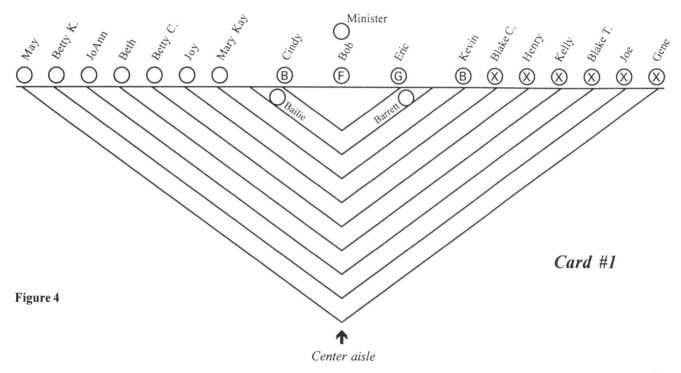

Figure 4

Card #1

Center aisle

Line-up coming in

Gene
Joe
Blake T.
Kelly
Henry
Blake C.

May
Betty K.
JoAnn
Beth
Betty C.
Joy - matron of honor
Mary Kay - maid of honor
Bailie - flower girl; Barrett -
    ring bearer
Cindy - bride; Bob - father

Card #2

Line-up going out

Cindy - bride; Eric - groom
Bailie - Barrett
Mary Kay - Kevin
Joy - Blake C.
Betty C. - Henry
Beth - Kelly
JoAnn - Blake T.
Betty K. - Joe
May - Gene

Card #3

Figure 5: Sample Line-up Cards

Before you look at Figure 6, I would like to make several points. The bride can come down the aisle on her father's left or right arm. I like to see her on her father's left arm for two reasons: she is closest to her mother if she stops to give her a rose and a kiss, and her father is between her and the groom, so when he leaves her, he can give her a kiss and give her arm to the groom. The only part that is tricky is the father must back up several steps in order not to step on the bride's train. Of course, the minister will decide on which position he likes best.

In the diagrams, you will notice that I have made a cross mark in the center of the groomsmen's circles. This will show you at a glance which circles are groomsmen and which are bridesmaids. You will see how that helps you when you make your diagrams. You will move circles around quite a bit when trying to get a good balance when bridesmaids are on both sides.

Finally, you will see in Figure 6 that the recessional is different when you have the bridesmaids on both sides. The bridesmaids on the groom's side must cross over in the center before they take the groomsmen's right arms. This is necessary in order that all the couples recess on the same side. This will make all bridesmaids come out on the bride's side of the church.

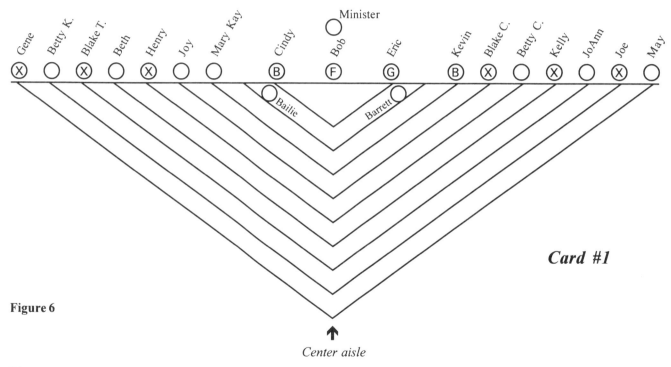

ALTAR – Bridesmaids on both sides

Minister

Gene · Betty K. · Blake T. · Beth · Henry · Joy · Mary Kay · Cindy · Bob · Eric · Kevin · Blake C. · Betty C. · Kelly · JoAnn · Joe · May

Bailie

Barrett

Card #1

Figure 6

↑
Center aisle

Line-up coming in

Joe
Gene
Kelly
Blake T.
Blake C.
Henry
Betty K.
May
Beth
JoAnn
Betty C.
Joy - matron of honor
Mary Kay - maid of honor

Card #2

Line-up going out

Cindy - Eric
Bailie - Barrett
Mary Kay - Kevin
Joy - Blake C.
Betty C. - Henry
Beth - Kelly
JoAnn - Blake T.
Betty K. - Joe
May - Gene

Card #3

Figure 7: Sample Line-up Cards

There are many ways to make up your diagrams, depending on how many attendants you have. We have already talked about the easiest diagram in which all the bridesmaids are on one side. Having a maid of honor and four bridesmaids is another easy arrangement. Here you have a maid of honor, two bridesmaids and two groomsmen on the bride's side, and the best man, two bridesmaids and two groomsmen on the groom's side. Here the wedding party is well-balanced. The attendants do not have to be placed in a straight line. The bridesmaids look very nice about three steps out from the groomsmen. If there are steps at the altar, the attendants can be placed on the steps. You will still have the same line-up. Here are three diagrams you might use:

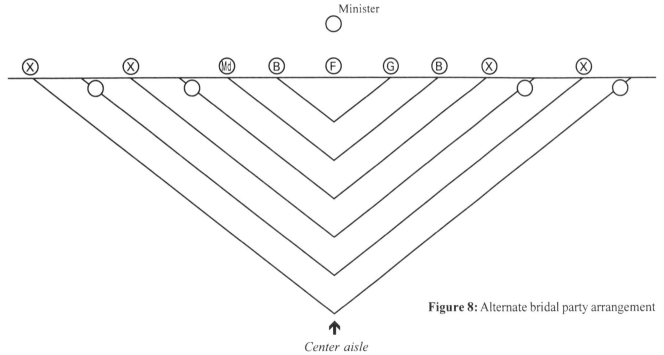

Figure 8: Alternate bridal party arrangement

Center aisle

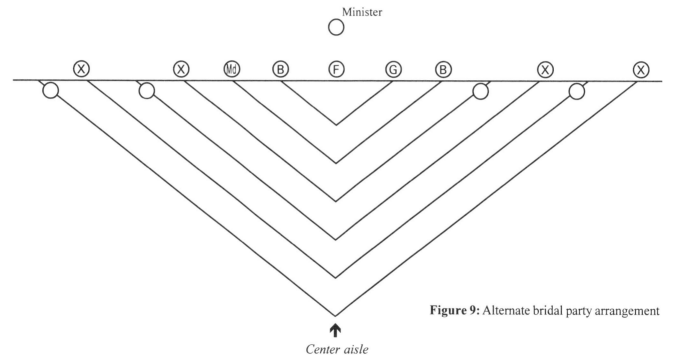

Figure 9: Alternate bridal party arrangement

Center aisle

The third diagram is nice when the attendants are going out of the church in couples from each side. There would be no crossing over for bridesmaids already on the bride's side when they reach the center aisle.

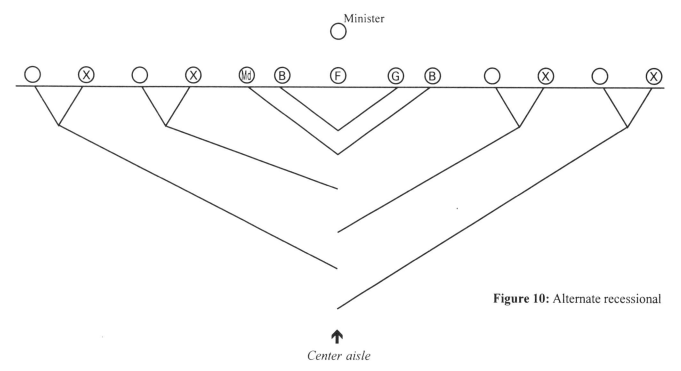

Figure 10: Alternate recessional

Minister

Center aisle

In The Figure 10 diagram, the attendants may go into the church single file and come out as couples. There are so many variations depending upon the bride's desires. Your main objective is to line up the wedding party to the bride's satisfaction *before* the rehearsal. With the bride's help, start drawing circles to represent the people in the wedding party. Keep moving and adjusting until you are satisfied with the line-up. I have found that most of the time the diagram will not have to be adjusted at the rehearsal. Sometimes, we move a bridesmaid or groomsman because of height. A good diagram will be a great pay-off the night of the rehearsal. With the diagram and the answers to the questions you have asked, you are ready to make four 5x7 index cards with the following information:

CARD #1 - Make a diagram at the altar

CARD #2 - Line-up coming in - Processional

CARD #3 - Going out - Recessional

CARD #4 - Escorts

You should have the first three cards made up without any trouble. If necessary, look back where I gave you illustrations for these cards. We have not talked about card 4. The names of the groomsmen who will escort the grandmothers was given on the first form. From this information, you make up card 4.

Escorts

1. To escort groom's grandmothers
   Kelly and Henry
2. To escort bride's grandmothers
   Gene and Blake C.
3. To escort groom's mother
   Henry
4. To escort bride's mother
   Blake C.
5. Bride's mother will recess with husband
6. Groom's mother will recess with husband

Card #4

Figure 11: Sample Escort Card

• *Points to Remember and Mistakes to Avoid*

With the four cards filled out, you are ready for rehearsal. But before I talk about the rehearsal, I need to mention a few things about the minister, organist, video tape director and photographer. The minister certainly knows what he is doing, but sometimes he does not listen and understand when he is to enter with the groom and best man. If you have a solo after the mothers are seated, make sure the minister knows about the solo. In my experience, I have seen a minister, groom and best man enter before the solo. This can really mess up things; of course, this is a rare case, but it can happen. You have two choices in a situation like this. You can let the minister, groom and best man stand at the altar while the song is being sung, or start the groomsmen and bridesmaids down the aisle. I decided to send the wedding party down during the song. It was very pretty, but I do not like that to happen. I was trying to cover up for a mistake. So, talk with the minister before the ceremony to make sure he understands about the solos and whether the grandmothers are remaining in their pews at the end of the service. To signal the minister, I always raise my hand when the recessional is over and all honored guests have been escorted out of the church. In this way, the minister can raise his hand to the congregation signaling the end of the wedding.

You need to go over the music with the organist so you will understand what will be played for the mothers to come into the church, the solos, the procession of the attendants and the bride and father. You need to know if the hour will be chimed. Finally, you need to check watches to see that you are working on the exact same time. The difference of a few minutes can be important.

The video director must set up in the balcony. Sometimes, the lights are too dim and should be adjusted for the video director as well as the photographer. Check to be sure that the photographer knows that he is not to use flashbulbs in the church during the service. He has signed a contract explaining the church policies, but I have actually seen a photographer try to go up the aisle during the recessional to get a closer picture of the bride and groom. He must wait until the couple have arrived at the doorway.

As a director, you must be careful in bringing in the mothers. Remember the bride's mother is the *last* to come into the church, but the *first* to go out, right after the wedding party. I am addressing these incidents to help you watch for mistakes. Even though you have not made the mistakes yourself, you are still greatly affected by them. Here, communication is very important. A director must see that everyone involved in the wedding *fully* understands what they are doing. I am giving you some of my experiences so you can learn and keep these things from happening. Sometimes, you have only a few minutes to make a decision. Try to use good judgement. It seems we remember mistakes much more than the perfect weddings we have conducted. Hopefully, we profit from our mistakes.

Before we work through a rehearsal, I would like to address several additional points. The rehearsal must begin promptly at the appointed hour. A well-organized director will take one hour rehearsing. The bride and groom must contact every member of the wedding party to be sure they are at the church at the proper time. If one of the members of the wedding party will not be at the rehearsal, the director needs to know before hand; then the director can use a stand-in and inform the other members of the situation. The marriage license (obtained from the county court house probate office) should be brought to the rehearsal and left with the minister. The bride is expected to rehearse with the other members of the wedding party. Honored guests, such as the grandmothers, must participate in the rehearsal also.

- ### *Sample Rehearsal*

In the next few pages, I will take you step by step through a rehearsal using the cards and information received from the bride.

1. DIAGRAM CARD AT ALTAR

Invite all of the wedding party to sit in the first two pews of the church before asking the minister to have a word of prayer. After the prayer, encourage everyone to listen carefully so we can finish within the hour. Using the diagram card, place each member at the altar. When they are all in place, ask the bride to step out of her place and look at the line-up. If there are steps at the altar, you can place couples on them, or you might place the bridesmaids a few steps out from the groomsmen. Whatever you choose, you keep the same line-up unless you need to make an adjustment. If you make an adjustment, change it on your card now. When everything is satisfactory, ask the father to be seated with the bride's mother. Have each person look closely where they are standing so they can return to the same place. Ask one of the wedding committee members to put a small piece of tape where each person is standing. The tape will come up easily after the wedding. After this, instruct the bride and groom to turn to each other and walk to the back of the church. Instruct the ring bearer, flower girl and the attendants coming in couples in the same manner. Let each couple start recessing as the couple in front of them passes the third pew. Watch each couple to see if they stay in position until the couple in the center recesses down the aisle and if the bridesmaids on the groom's side cross in front of their groomsmen before taking their arms. You will work with each couple so that you know they are doing it right. The best man and maid of honor can see that the flower girl and the ring bearer leave together. They are cute whatever they do if they are well-behaved.

2. LINE-UP COMING IN - PROCESSIONAL

Using the line-up coming in card (2), line up the wedding party at the back of the church. After the minister, groom and best man take their positions at the altar, send each person down the aisle. Timing is very important. When the first groomsman is half way, send the next one. As the first groomsman is at the altar, the second groomsman is half way, start the third groomsman. This offers a nice spacing. Explain this to each groomsman as he is going down the aisle. He can watch to see if he is going too fast or slow. After the last groomsman is in place and looking to the back of the church, start the first bridesmaid. She should not go until you tap her on the back. When the first bridesmaid is about 3/4 of the way down the aisle, send the second bridesmaid, always reminding her to walk slowly. When *all* the bridesmaids are in place and looking to the back of the church, send the flower girl and/or ring bearer. When they are in place, explain to the father and bride that the music will stop, the chimes will sound the hour, and then slowly start them down the aisle. I walk down to the altar and before I turn them over to the minister, we talk about the way the attendants will stand. All attendants will face the back of the church as the bride comes down the aisle. They will keep their eyes on the bride, slowly pivoting to face the couple as the couple arrive at the altar. At this time, the minister takes over and goes through the wedding ceremony.

3. LINE-UP GOING OUT CARD - RECESSIONAL

After the minister finishes going through the ceremony, without help, the wedding party starts the recessional. Look at your card (3) to see if everyone is recessing correctly. This is almost the only time I need to refer to my card. After the recessional, meet the wedding party at the back of the church. Ask if there are any questions. At this time, talk to the groomsmen about their hands. At the altar, they may stand with their hands hanging loosely at their sides, clasped in front of them or behind their backs. Whatever is decided, all should stand the same way. Personally, I like their hands clasped in front, right over left.

4. ESCORT CARD

Finally, take your escort card (4) to show which groomsmen will escort grandmothers and mothers into the church. This does not necessarily mean these groomsmen will escort them out. Sometimes, we leave the grandmothers in the pews so they will be in place for pictures after the wedding. Also, the mothers may come out with their husbands. At this time, we will talk about how each will be escorted in and out. All of this information is on the card. Next, line up the grandmothers and mothers for practice. Instruct the groomsmen, bridesmaids, ring bearer, flower girl, bride, and father to line up behind the grandmothers and mothers. After the groomsmen have escorted the grandmothers and mothers, instruct them to return and take their places in the line-up. This will be the third time the attendants have gone through this procedure. Before you begin the processional, the minister, groom and best man enter from the back of the altar and take their positions. This time, go through the entire service just like the day of the wedding. If you have taught the whole wedding party well, you should not have to use your cards on the wedding day. On the wedding day, you can focus on the timing and spacing of the attendants. You can be in the back of the church to help the groomsmen if they need your service. You can watch to see if the church is filling up with guests properly. Finally, you are there to take care of any problem that might occur.

Before the rehearsal is over, I like to go over several things with the groomsmen. 1.) Do not ask guests whether they would like to sit on the bride's or groom's side. If they request a side, by all means seat them there, but try to keep the sides filled up as evenly as possible. 2.) You may extend either your right or your left arm to escort guests down the aisle. 3.) If you see a guest with a camera, tell them there is no picture taking during the service. 4.) Try to seat the guests as quickly as possible so that a long line of waiting guests will not form. 5.) Do not seat any guests after the mothers are escorted to their pews. Remember the mother of the bride is the last person seated. She signals the beginning of the wedding. After informing the groomsmen of these points, they can take their places in the line-up. Ask if there are any questions. Remember, a good rehearsal will make the wedding day a lot easier.

Before the wedding party leaves, you must make sure they understand they are to be at the church two hours before the wedding. The groomsmen must be dressed and ready for pictures. The bride, bridesmaids and mothers will be ready to put on their dresses. If there are two hours before the wedding, you have plenty of time to solve problems if they come up.

• *Sample Wedding*

Picture this sample wedding as we go through it step-by-step. In this sample, I have used some extras such as a flower girl, ring bearer, giving of roses, and the unity candle, etc. You might not have all of these, as there are variations in all weddings. For instance, in some ceremonies the minister, groom and best man come down the aisle, or in other cases, the groomsmen come from behind the altar with the groom. I am going to go through a typical ceremony. If you understand how to direct this wedding, you can make adjustments and adapt it to the particular wedding you are directing.

This wedding is in a church at 7:00 in the evening. There are six bridesmaids, a maid of honor, flower girl, ring bearer, best man and six groomsmen. The reception will be held at a country club. Approximately three-hundred guests have responded yes to the RSVP cards, therefore it is not necessary to have extra groomsmen. Before the rehearsal, you made your four cards; now you are ready to direct the wedding.

Before the Wedding

5:00 - The bride, bridesmaids, and mothers arrive at the church and go to the designated room to dress. The groom and his groomsmen must stay in a designated room until the photographer comes in for them. They should be dressed so the wedding committee member can check their attire and pin on boutonnieres. I find this procedure takes time. If the job has not been done by a florist, the committee member may continue to help with the flowers. If anything goes wrong, there is time for the wedding committee member to make adjustments.

5:30 - The photographer starts with the pictures of the groom and groomsmen so that the groomsmen are finished in plenty of time for escorting guests. All other members of the wedding party should be at the church, dressed and ready for pictures.

6:00 - The pictures of the bride with her parents are taken.

Wedding

6:15 - All groomsmen are in position at the church entrance with the wedding director. At this time, the committee members are with the bride, bridesmaids, and mothers ready to assist the director.

6:30 - Groomsmen have started escorting guests, and the organist is playing selections of nuptial music. Candles are to be lighted by two groomsmen or alcotyles unless the florist has been instructed to do this job. It is not good to use groomsmen if at all possible, for it takes them away from ushering.

6:50 - The groomsmen escort the grandmothers to their seats. Each grandmother on the groom's side is escorted separately and they are seated behind where the groom's mother is to sit. The grandmothers on the bride's side are escorted in the same manner.

6:57 - The groom's mother is slowly escorted to her seat on the front pew on the right side. She and her husband light the candle on the right side of the unity candle. Her husband can escort her or follow behind. I prefer her husband to escort her to the altar and then seat her in the pew.

7:00 - The bride's mother is slowly escorted to her seat on the front pew on the left side. Before she is seated, she and her husband go to the altar and light the candle on the left side of the unity candle. She is the last person seated before the beginning of the wedding. The groomsmen stop ushering and get in position for the processional. The wedding director instructs the late comers to seat themselves down the side aisles.

Mary sings "O Perfect Love"

When the processional music starts, the minister, groom and best man enter from behind the altar to their positions.

When the minister, groom and best man are in their places and looking to the back of the church, the groomsmen go slowly down the aisle in pairs.

After the groomsmen are in place standing with their hands clasped in front, right over left, the bridesmaids go slowly down the aisle one at a time.

All of the bridesmaids are in place before the maid of honor goes slowly down the aisle.

After the maid of honor is in place and looking to the back of the church, the flower girl and ring bearer go down the aisle together. They could go separately if the bride wishes, but I find they are less reluctant when the two go together.

The music stops, and the organist chimes the hour. All attendants look at the bride as she enters the church. The music starts again. The director straightens the bride's train, and the bride escorted on her father's left arm, slowly goes down the aisle to her smiling groom.

As the bride and her father go down the aisle, the mother stands. The bride stops and gives her a kiss and a rose. As they process, the attendants slowly turn to face the altar.

The father stands between the bride and groom until the minister says, "Who giveth this woman to be married to this man?" The father replies, "Her mother and I." The father kisses the bride and places her arm on the groom's arm. The father should step back to avoid stepping on the bride's train. Then he sits beside the bride's mother.

The best man and maid of honor move in closer to the bride and groom. The maid of honor gives her flowers to the bridesmaid nearest her, and the bride gives her flowers to the maid of honor before the couple take their vows and exchange rings.

The groom helps the bride to kneel at the altar. The soloist sings "The Lord's Prayer."

The couple use the lighted candles to light the unity candle in the center. They may blow out the other two candles in a symbolic gesture of the unification of two families and two hearts. The minister closes with a final prayer.

The bride and groom kiss. She takes her flowers from the maid of honor who straightens her train. The couple stop to give the groom's mother a kiss and a rose. The couple recesses down the aisle followed by the attendants.

As the last couple in the wedding party get about three pews down the aisle, the father of the bride steps into the aisle and extends his arm to his wife and they follow the wedding party. The bride's parents are followed by the groom's in the same manner.

The grandmothers remain in their pews so they can be ready when the wedding party comes back for pictures.

The entire wedding party goes out of the church and reenters from the side door for pictures as soon as the guests have half emptied the church.

The wedding is over. The wedding committee members stay during picture taking. They check the room to be sure the wedding party has removed all personal items. This is important, for the custodian will be locking the church in a few hours. The florist removes all decorations. The flowers should be removed unless they are left to be used in the church.

This ends the responsibility of the director and wedding committee members at the church. They have helped fulfill, according to the church's approval, one of the most beautiful, sacred and important services of worship. We know from the Bible how much our Lord enjoyed weddings. In fact, He performed the first miracle at a wedding. What a precious moment it is to see two people come together in God's presence to receive His blessings and walk together with Him through life.

These are the guidelines to use my method of directing a wedding. I find if you prepare yourself well, you can have a well organized rehearsal and a perfect wedding. You can take this plan and adapt it according to various church rituals. I have conducted weddings in all churches and have found they all have most of the same basic needs.

• *Directing a Wedding Reception*

Many wedding receptions are larger and more elaborate than they used to be. Here, I will lead you step by step through the way I direct a wedding reception.

Leave the church during picture taking to go to the reception. Once there, familiarize yourself with the room. If there is a band playing, go directly to the leader and instruct him or her to announce the newlyweds when they arrive. Give him or her a signal when the couple arrives. If you are satisfied with the way the reception is going, return to the club's entrance to wait for the wedding party. Keep the whole wedding party together as you arrive on the dance floor. The band leader announces the newlyweds, and they dance the first dance together. Afterwards, they are joined by the bride's and the groom's parents. As the bride and father dance, the groom and the bride's mother dance. The bride's and the groom's parents exchange partners and dance. Finally, they are joined by the bridesmaids and groomsmen. After the wedding party has danced, the guests feel free to dance. The dancing has given the photographer a chance to get some very good pictures before bride, groom, and parents are greeted by their guests.

Work very closely with the photographer at the reception. About a half hour after the bride and groom have been mingling with the guests, direct them to the wedding cake. The photographer takes pictures of them cutting the cake, feeding the cake to each other and drinking wine.

After these pictures, the wedding cake should be served immediately. I have attended receptions, when the wedding cake was not served until two-thirds of the guests had left. This is a bad mistake. Be sure this does not happen, as the wedding cake is a very special part of the reception. Make sure that you have a person at the cake table to see that the guests have a piece of your wedding cake. A tale is told that if a single woman takes a piece of wedding cake and puts it on her night table, she will dream about the man she will marry. A sweet elderly lady who never married told me that she took a piece of wedding cake home from every ceremony she attended. I never knew if she dreamed about a man. Still, it is a nice story.

About two hours into the reception, ask the band leader to invite all the single women to the dance floor so the bride can throw her bouquet to them. The one who catches it is supposed to be the next to marry. Afterwards, all single gentlemen are invited to try to catch the bride's garter which the groom has removed from the bride's leg. The gentleman who catches the garter is supposed to be the next to marry.

A wedding reception with a band usually lasts about three hours. After the guests have eaten, they seem to stay longer to enjoy dancing. When the crowd is thinning out a great deal, it is time for the couple to change clothes for departure. When they are through, they come back to dance. The band leader announces that the bride and groom are about to depart, and all guests are invited to the entrance of the club before the couple runs to their car or limousine. The guests laugh and shout their good-byes as the newlyweds duck their heads to dodge showers of rose petals. They climb into the limousine and wave as they leave the crowd. Carefree and happy, they start their journey through life together. As a director, you will be tired but happy you have been a part of helping two people start their new life.

● *Final Points to Remember*

To the mother and bride: I would like to remind you to focus on your objective, to have a beautiful wedding. Do not see how much money you can spend and how elaborate the wedding can be. In the years I have been involved in directing weddings, the ones that stand out in my mind are the very simple, non-flashy weddings. Do not put on a show. I have seen some parents have an extremely elaborate and showy wedding which was not outstanding and looked like a stage production. They just missed the point. A simple, elegant and beautiful wedding correctly performed can be a lasting and beautiful worship experience not only for the bride and groom, but to the wedding party and all the guests. Think seriously about this when planning your wedding.

I hope I have helped you. If you use this book as a guide and work through each topic step by step, you will cover each item needed for your wedding. I know there will be many questions you would like answered. Your answers will be found through the important numbers you have made into a book. Do not hesitate to call the church office, the wedding committee and the services you have hired for your wedding. They will be able to answer all your questions. Remember, they are all interested in making your wedding a happy and beautiful occasion. Let them work for you. Spend time together and look forward to the upcoming wedding. Weddings should be fun!

Now, to the wedding director, I would like to emphasize several points. Again, keep an open and thorough communication with the bride and mother. Understand their wishes completely. Make your four cards from the information you have received. Prepare yourself well before the rehearsal. At the rehearsal, teach your wedding party so well that they will not have to depend on you the day of the wedding. One of the most important points to remember is, as you rehearse, watch the timing and the spacing of your attendants. Be alert to make any last minute decisions to the best of your ability. Above all, you need to be relaxed. You have worked hard, now enjoy carrying out your plans.

There are so many ways to plan and direct a wedding. You could spend months reading material written on the subject. I have spent years living with my subject to finally combine all my ideas and experiences together to come up with this simple plan to benefit interested people. I hate to see people worry over plans that can be easy and enjoyable.

● *Lasting Marriages and Sacred Ceremonies*

In closing, let me try to answer two questions that brides have asked me through the years. What do you think are some of the most important ingredients in a successful marriage? And why do you enjoy directing weddings? To the first question I say, many have written about the road of life. My feelings are that marriage is a journey down a dirt road. As a couple walks down the road, they need the Lord walking with them. Sometimes they will find the road is smooth, and other times bumpy. The road is filled with hills (pleasures, happiness, joy, excitement) and deep valleys (distress, anger, sickness, disappointments, sorrow) and curves in the road so you can not see what faces you on the other side. Some days are sunny, and some days are rainy, but you must enjoy the sunny days and weather the rainy ones. Some of the ingredients you will need are love, faith, loyalty and trust, as well as being needed. All of these are important, but above all should be communication, which can be verbal or quietly spending time together, receiving a smile, a touch or a kiss. In this world we live in, I do not think we can have too much communication. These are some of the most important ingredients in a successful marriage. Now for the second question—how I feel about directing weddings.

I enjoy directing because I think weddings are one of the most beautiful and sacred ceremonies in our churches. Throughout the Bible, our Lord speaks many times of weddings. What a happy occasion it is when two people in love are standing before the Lord, relatives and guests to take their vows to live together until they are parted by death. Most of all, life is full of *giving* and *receiving*. I like to *give* my talents to help brides and grooms prepare for a very exciting and beautiful day in their lives. In return, I *receive* the joy, happiness and satisfaction of being a part of the beginning of their life's journey.

Final Suggestions

For some final suggestions, I have included three helpful subjects that can enhance your wedding and create lasting keepsakes: drying rose petals, creating children's heirloom dresses, and preserving wedding dresses.

● *Drying Rose Petals*

Traditionally, rice was thrown when newlyweds departed for their honeymoon. Rice was believed to ensure happiness and fertility. Today, rice and birdseed are being replaced by silk or dried rose petals. Here is an easy method for drying petals.

Take three long gift boxes and place them on top of your clothes dryer. Take the roses from your garden, pull each petal and place them in one of the boxes. You only want one layer of roses in a box. If you have more than one layer, they will not dry well and may begin to mold. Stir the roses with your hands every day. You can see the stages they go through in the drying process each day. In one week, the roses should be completely dried and ready to put in a Zip-loc bag. If you like you can put three or four drops of rose oil into the bag. Flower oils can be found at most craft or gift stores. Do not use much, for the oils are very strong in odor.

When you pick new fresh petals, do not mix them with the petals you have started drying. This is the reason you should have three boxes. You can have different groups of petals drying at three different stages. Just be sure to stir each box daily. You can tell when the roses are thoroughly dry. Even though it only takes three or four days, I like to keep them in the box a week to be sure they are dry before putting them in a bag. They are wonderful to use in a flower girl's basket or to throw at the bride and groom when they depart. Also, take the flowers used at the reception and dry them in the same way. Add any flower oil to the petals. Place some dried flowers in a pretty white handkerchief and tie it up with a bow of ribbon. Give them to your bridesmaids, close friends or some older women that mean a lot to you in your life. They make wonderful and thoughtful gifts which will be treasured long after your wedding.

- ### *Children's Heirloom Dresses*

When my first granddaughter, Erin, was two years old, I decided to learn how to smock. Since I was twelve years old, I have always loved to embroidery. I spent hours smocking and embroidering, but I did not feel comfortable about putting my dresses together. I did not think they would look professional, so I found a very talented person to put together the dresses I designed, after I had finished the handwork. My dresses are batise, full of imported lace, smocking and embroidering. They are beautiful and perfect for flower girl and junior bridesmaid dresses. If made tea length, they can be worn for several years. Think about heirloom dresses when you plan attire for your young attendants.

When my first granddaughter outgrew the dresses I made, my second granddaughter, Bailie, inherited them. It is wonderful how they can be passed down from one child to the next in the family. After the children have grown up, the dresses need to be cleaned and preserved.

The steps in preserving heirloom dresses are as follows. Wash the dress in Woolite or any mild detergent. Rinse the garment three or four times. It is very important that all of the soap be completely rinsed out. Dry the dress thoroughly. Check to be sure it is completely clean and without stains. Do not iron it. Stuff the dress into a large glass mason jar. Dress sizes up to a four will fit in a large mason jar. Any kind of larger glass jars can be used for larger dresses. I like to use glass jars because you can see the dress, so you do not need to open it. I store my jars in a large box that is divided into sections. The dresses will keep well until one day, many years later, another little girl will come along ready to wear the dress in the jar.

- ### *Wedding Gown Preservation*

From the time little girls are old enough to play with bride dolls and see pictures of their mothers in a wedding dress, many envision wearing the same white gown. There is a disappointment when the dress is removed from storage to discover a stained, yellow and crumpled dress. Don't give up, sometimes it can be restored.

When I was married forty-two years ago, I wore a wedding gown of de-Venice lace, nylon marquisette and imported illusion with accordion pleated ruffles which ended in a cathedral train. My mother had my dress cleaned after the wedding and placed in a large bag. The bag was put in a garment box, tightly sealed, and placed in a closet. Twenty-five years later, when my first daughter, Joy, was preparing to get married, we took the dress out of the box. I found the material had turned from snow white to a beautiful candlelight color. It was in good shape, but all the pearls had turned dark.

After taking the seed pearls off, I took it to an area dry cleaner. Because it was so old, they sent it to the National Institute of Dry Cleaners in Maryland. The institute can take care of aging materials. The process used by the institute is one of analyzing the fabric and dye to be sure of fiber content and any other factors that may determine how the dress should be cleaned. If they can clean it, they guarantee everything except artificial materials, such as pearls. The dress turned out beautifully. After it came back from Maryland, my mother and I spent seventy hours sewing new pearls on the dress! When my daughter's wedding was over, the dress was sent back to Maryland, cleaned and boxed once again. Who knows? Maybe my granddaughters will wear it some day.

Today's gowns are not as preservable as those of the past because most modern gowns are made of man-made fibers. They will disintegrate over a period of time, but some can be restored. It takes a more delicate procedure because man-made fibers are less durable. When your wedding is over, there are several things you must remember. Your dress cannot be put away with perfume and perspiration on it. It should be checked for stains, tears and snags before it is cleaned. If properly boxed, it could last for fifty years. You will find area cleaners who will help you with wedding gown preservation. It is wonderful to have a keepsake in the family. Maybe you have a wedding dress that you are thinking of restoring. Give it a try; it might work!

Notes

Notes

Notes

Notes

Notes

Notes

Notes

Notes

Notes

Notes

Notes

WESLEY UNITED METHODIST CHURCH
3425 WEST 30th STREET
INDIANAPOLIS, IND. 46222

Wesley United Methodist Church
3425 W. 30th Street
Indianapolis, IN 46222

DEMCO